THE NERVOUS SYSTEM

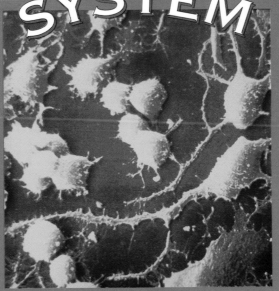

A TRUE BOOK

by

Darlene R. Stille

Children's Press®
A Division of Grolier Publishing

New York London Hong Kong Sydney
Danbury, Connecticut

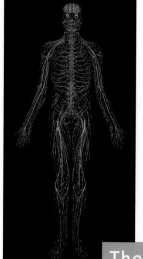

Reading Consultant
Linda Cornwell
Learning Resource Consultant
Indiana Department of Education

Science Consultant
Ronald W. Schwizer, Ph.D.
Science Chair
Poly Prep Country Day School
Brooklyn, New York

The nervous
system

Library of Congress Cataloging-in-Publication Data

Stille, Darlene R.
    The Nervous system / by Darlene R. Stille.
        p. cm.—(A True book)
    Includes bibliographical references and index.
        Summary: Describes the various parts of the nervous system
and explains how sensory messages are sent back and forth
through nerves between the brain and the body.
        ISBN 0-516-20445-9 (lib. bdg.)   0-516-26270-X (pbk.)
        1. Nervous system—Juvenile literature. [1. Nervous system.]
I. Title. II. Series.
QP361.5.S85   1997
612. 8—dc21
                                                                96-29738
                                                                     CIP
                                                                      AC

Printed in China

Contents

The Body's Computer Network 5

The Parts of the Nervous System 9

The Brain 13

The Spinal Cord 19

Nerve Cells 24

Ins and Outs of Nerve Talk 30

Nerves and Muscles 38

To Find Out More 44

Important Words 46

Index 47

Meet the Author 48

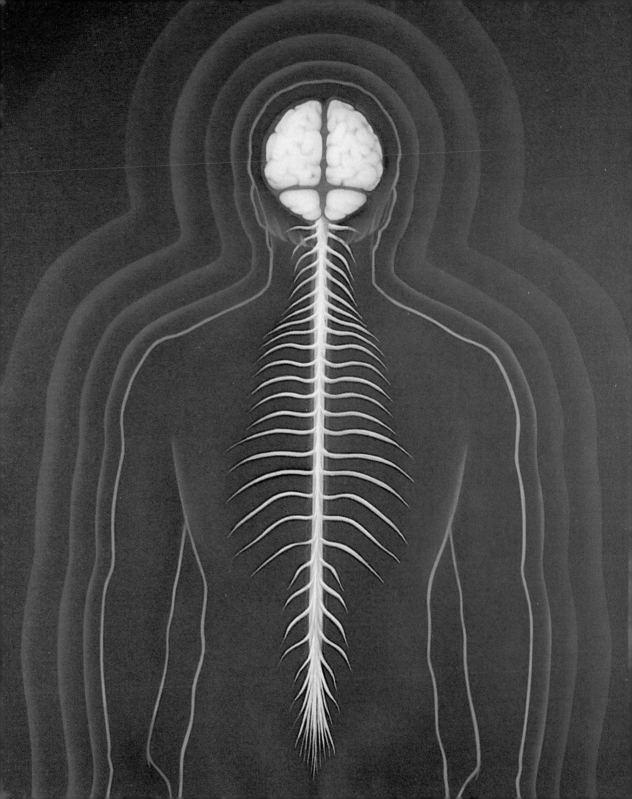

The Body's Computer Network

People often compare the brain and nervous system to a powerful computer network. They think of the brain as the central computer and the nervous system as the wires that carry the information.

Computers are wonderful. They can do many tasks. They

No computer can match the amazing abilities of the human brain.

work at lightning speed. They run programs that allow us to draw, write papers, look up information, and even play games. Computers also control complex systems, from car engines to spacecraft.

But no computer has anything like the power of the human brain. The brain can think. It stores all our memories and experiences and makes links between them. The brain decides what pictures we will draw, what we will write about, what information we need to look up, and how to win the games we play.

And the brain controls systems far more complex than a car engine—or even a spacecraft. The brain controls our heartbeat, breathing, and all the body systems that keep us alive.

The brain is the center of human emotions.

But more than that, the brain is the center of our emotions. The brain and nervous system allow us to get angry or jealous, and allow us to feel love and friendship. Many people believe it is the brain and nervous system that make human beings unique.

The Parts of the Nervous System

Like a central computer, the brain controls all the parts of the nervous system. The brain is located in the head and is protected by thick skull bones.

At the bottom of the brain, just above the neck, is the brain stem. This area connects

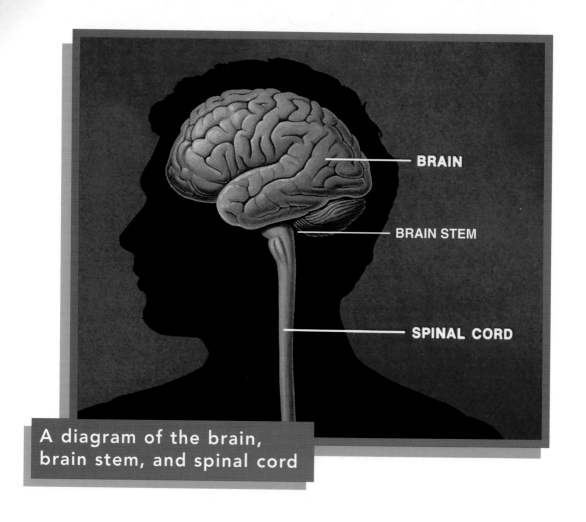

BRAIN

BRAIN STEM

SPINAL CORD

A diagram of the brain,
brain stem, and spinal cord

the brain to the spinal cord.
Together, the brain and spinal
cord make up the central
nervous system.

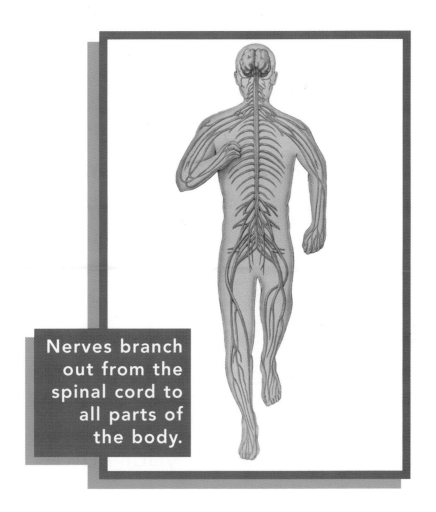

Nerves branch out from the spinal cord to all parts of the body.

From the spinal cord, nerves branch out to all parts of the body. This network of nerves is called the peripheral nervous system. It handles signals between the central nervous system and distant parts of the body.

Finally, there is a part of the nervous system that acts as your "automatic pilot." It is called the autonomic nervous system. It controls your automatic body functions—the things you never think about, such as your heartbeat, your food digestion, and your breathing.

The Brain

The brain weighs about 3 pounds (1.4 kilograms). It is soft and grayish-pink, and it has many folds and creases. The brain has several parts. Each part has special jobs to do.

The largest part of the brain is called the cerebrum. Different parts of the cerebrum send

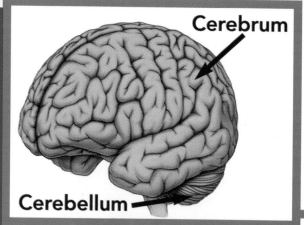

Cerebrum

Cerebellum

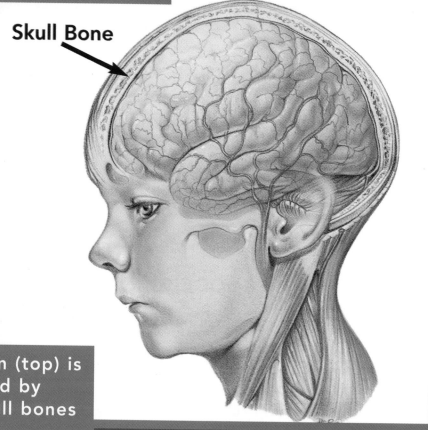

Skull Bone

The brain (top) is protected by thick skull bones (bottom).

and receive messages from different parts of the body. For example, some parts receive signals from the eyes and ears, allowing us to see and hear. Some parts control our muscle movements. And parts of the cerebrum control our ability to learn, create, and remember.

Below and behind the cerebrum is an area of the brain that is responsible for balance and coordination. It is called the cerebellum.

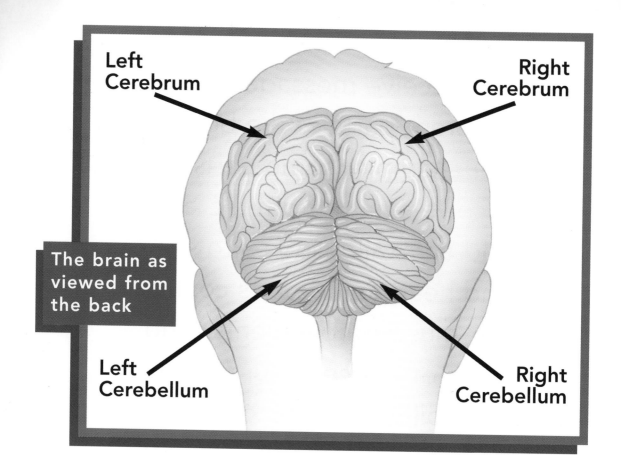

Left Cerebrum

Right Cerebrum

The brain as viewed from the back

Left Cerebellum

Right Cerebellum

The cerebrum and cerebellum are divided into two halves. The right half controls the left side of the body and the left half controls the right side of the body.

The brain stem connects the cerebrum with the spinal cord. But the brain stem is more than just a connection. It controls all the automatic functions of the autonomic nervous system.

An injury to a specific part of the brain can cause problems with the body functions controlled by that part of the brain. For example, an injury to the area of the brain that controls vision could cause blindness.

Brain Mapping

Different areas of the brain control different body functions. Scientists learned this by studying people whose brains had been damaged by injury or disease.

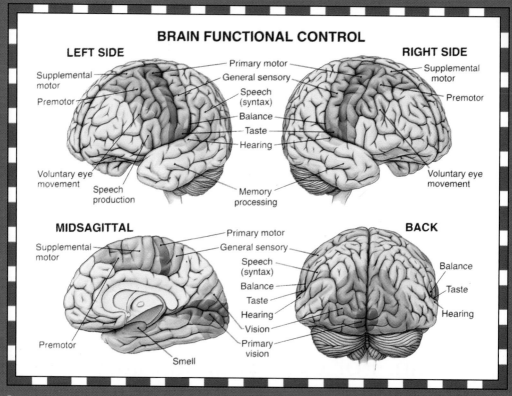

BRAIN FUNCTIONAL CONTROL

LEFT SIDE

Supplemental motor
Premotor
Voluntary eye movement
Speech production

Primary motor
General sensory
Speech (syntax)
Balance
Taste
Hearing
Memory processing

RIGHT SIDE

Supplemental motor
Premotor
Voluntary eye movement

MIDSAGITTAL

Supplemental motor
Premotor
Smell

Primary motor
General sensory
Speech (syntax)
Balance
Taste
Hearing
Vision
Primary vision

BACK

Balance
Taste
Hearing

After studying many people, scientists were able to make a map of the brain. The map shows where the control areas for speech, vision, memory, and other skills are located.

The Spinal Cord

The spinal cord is a bundle of nerves that begins at the brain stem and runs down the back. The spinal cord is protected by the backbone.

The spinal cord is the link between the brain and muscles and organs. Sensory nerves in the spinal cord send

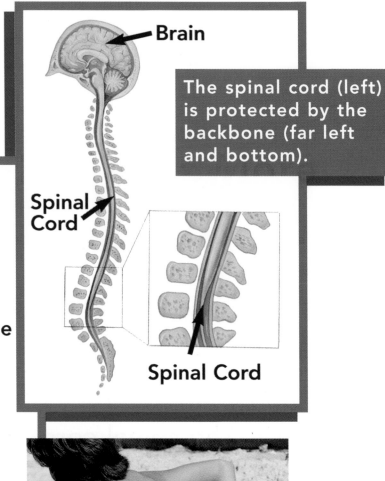

Brain

The spinal cord (left) is protected by the backbone (far left and bottom).

Spinal Cord

Spinal Cord

Backbone

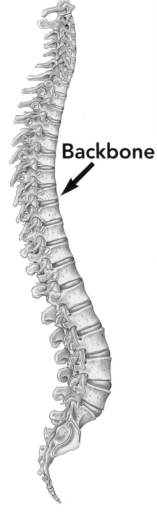

messages about the sense of touch to the brain. Motor nerves in the spinal cord send messages from the brain instructing certain muscles to move.

Injuries to the spinal cord can cause paralysis by cutting the lines of communication to the muscles. If damaged, nerve cells in the spinal cord do not grow back. The higher up on the spinal cord the injury is, the more body parts

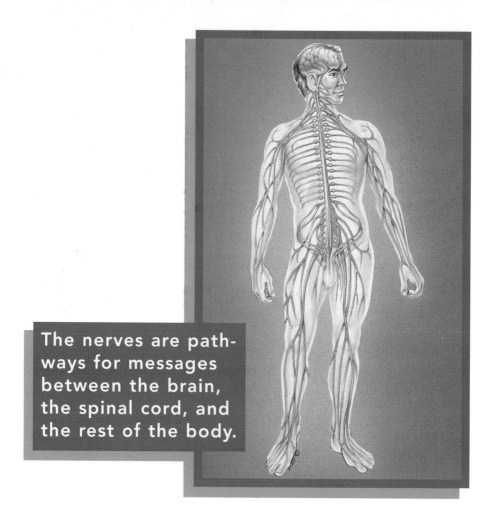

The nerves are path-
ways for messages
between the brain,
the spinal cord, and
the rest of the body.

are affected. An injury low in
the spinal cord may paralyze
the legs. An injury high up in
the neck area can cause

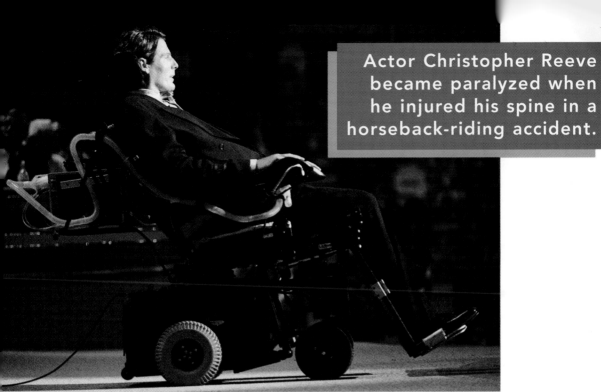

Actor Christopher Reeve became paralyzed when he injured his spine in a horseback-riding accident.

paralysis from the neck down, including arms and legs.

Automobile and diving accidents cause many spinal-cord injuries. Medical researchers are searching for better ways to treat injured spinal cords.

Nerve Cells

The brain and spinal cord contain billions of nerve cells. From a nerve cell body, fibers reach out like long fingers. Fibers called axons send out nerve signals. Fibers called dendrites receive signals. Each nerve cell has one cell body, one axon, and several dendrites.

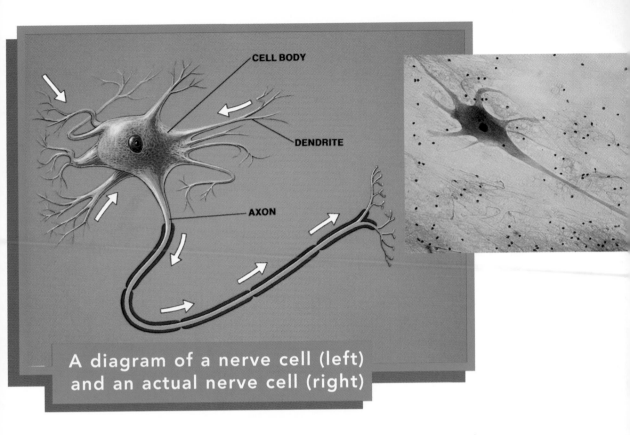

CELL BODY

DENDRITE

AXON

A diagram of a nerve cell (left) and an actual nerve cell (right)

The nerve fibers extend throughout the body, and each fiber can have hundreds of branches. Dendrites are very short, just a tiny fraction of an inch. Axons can be more than 3 feet (0.9 meters) long.

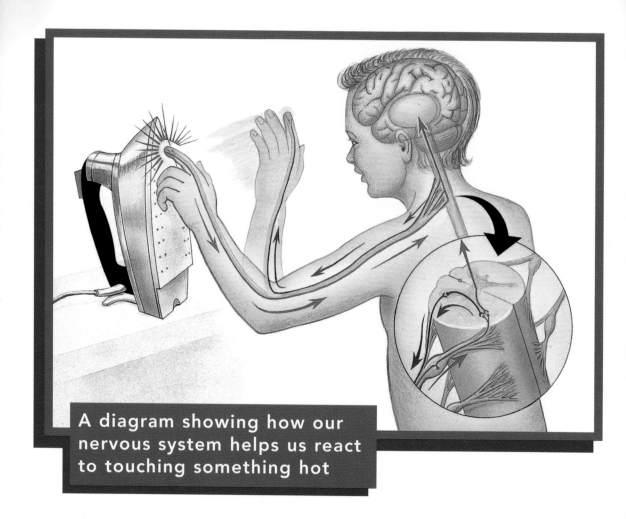

A diagram showing how our nervous system helps us react to touching something hot

All kinds of messages travel along nerve fibers. The nerves send a pain message from your finger to your brain if you touch a hot iron. Other nerves then send a message from your brain to the muscles in your arm to pull your hand away.

To do all these complex tasks, there are different types of nerve cells. Special nerve cells in the eyes, ears, skin, and other sense organs receive messages from the outside world. These are called sensory nerve cells. They pass the information to the brain or spinal cord. Motor nerve cells then

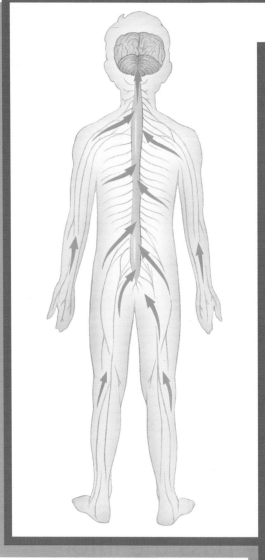
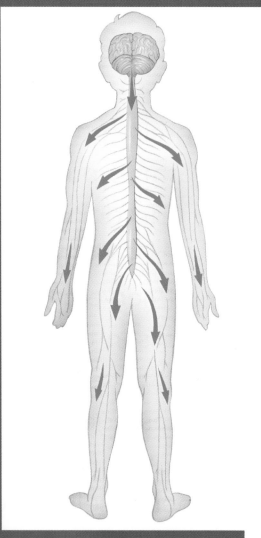

Sensory nerve cells send signals from the senses to the central nervous system (left). Motor nerve cells send signals from the central nervous system to the muscles and organs (right).

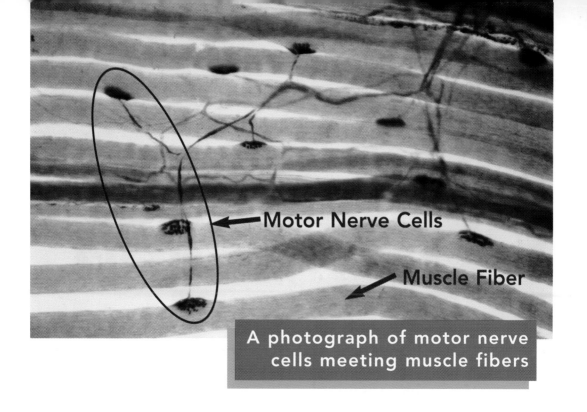

Motor Nerve Cells

Muscle Fiber

A photograph of motor nerve cells meeting muscle fibers

send messages back from the central nervous system telling the muscles and other organs how to react. This reaction could be contraction of a muscle or the production of an important chemical by an organ.

Ins and Outs of Nerve Talk

Our bodies and minds function in complex ways because our nerves "talk" to one another. They talk through the axons and the dendrites.

The tip of an axon from one nerve always lies close to a dendrite from another nerve. A message sent out

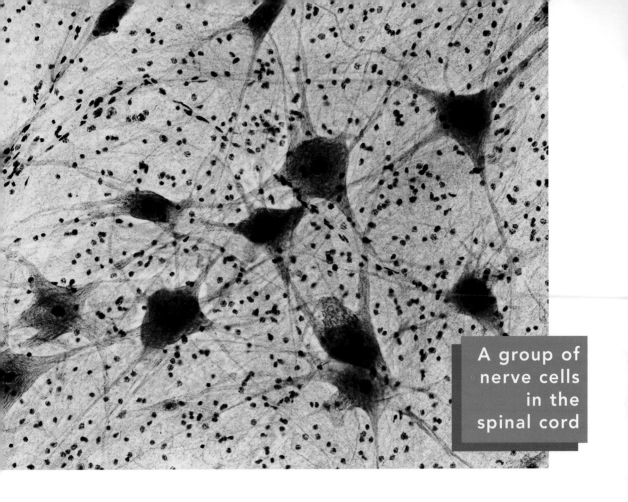

from a nerve cell body
through an axon gets picked
up by a dendrite, is passed
on to its nerve cell body, and
relayed through its axon. This

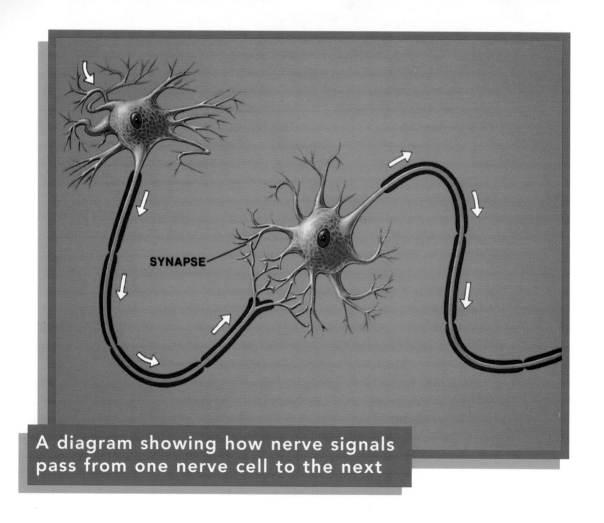

SYNAPSE

A diagram showing how nerve signals pass from one nerve cell to the next

continues until the message reaches its final destination, usually an organ, the brain, or a muscle.

If something touches your skin, your brain knows it instantly. This is because touching stimulates sensory nerves in your skin and causes them to "fire off" a message.

When you are touched, sensory nerves in your skin send a message to your brain.

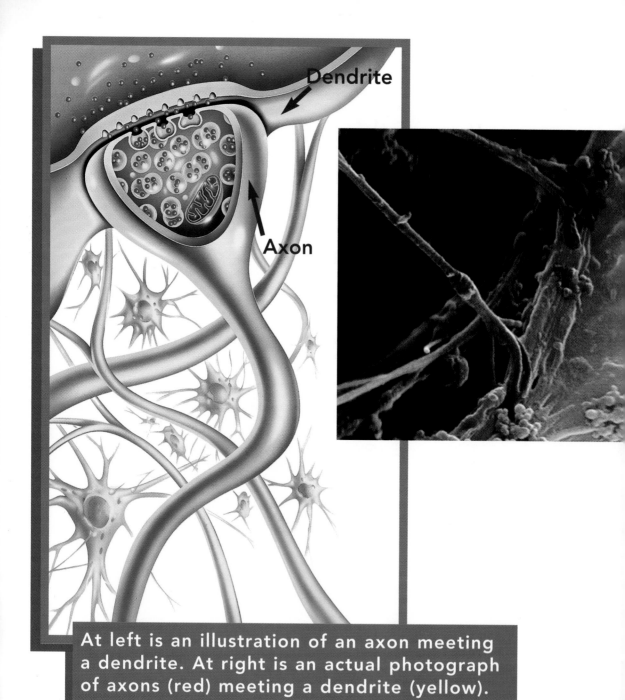

Dendrite

Axon

At left is an illustration of an axon meeting a dendrite. At right is an actual photograph of axons (red) meeting a dendrite (yellow).

But getting a message from an axon to a dendrite is harder than it sounds. Axons and dendrites never actually touch! The nerve message must travel across the gap between them.

To make the leap, the axon releases a chemical that carries the message across the gap. When the chemical reaches the dendrite, it causes an electrical impulse to shoot along the dendrite, and the nerve message continues through the cell body and down the axon of the next cell.

Some axons are wrapped in fatty material—just as phone wire is wrapped in plastic coating to provide insulation. This fatty coating protects the nerve tissue. In a disease called multiple sclerosis, the fatty coating disappears. Then the nerves cannot carry signals properly. This causes problems with muscle movements. Scientists are looking for a cure for this disease.

A cross-section of a normal axon coated with fatty material (right) and axons damaged by multiple sclerosis (below)

Nerves and Muscles

Nerves control all our muscle movements. Some movements happen so quickly that we do not have time to think about them. These are called reflex reactions.

The best-known reflex is called the knee-jerk reaction. Doctors often use this as a

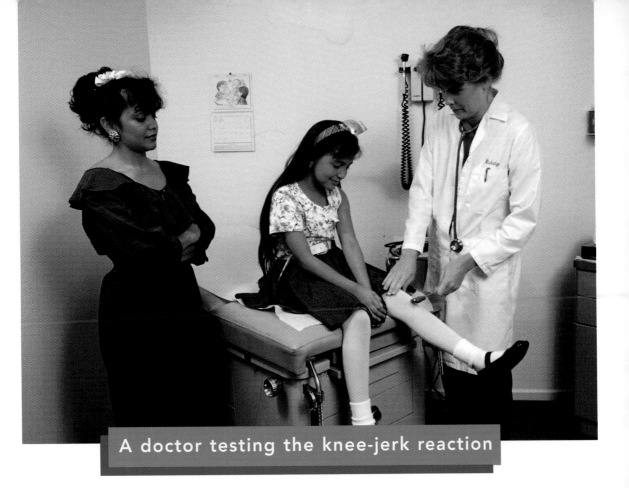

A doctor testing the knee-jerk reaction

reflex test. The doctor hits the patient's knee with a small rubber hammer, and the patient's leg jerks. The patient has no control over this.

What happens is that nerves in the knee sense the blow from the hammer and send a message to nerve cells in the spinal cord. The response is instantly routed back through a motor nerve, telling the knee to jerk. The brain never gets involved. Such fast reactions help us react quickly to avoid pain and serious injury.

But other muscle movements are not so simple. Just

Your brain and nervous system allow you to do complex tasks like learning a dance.

think how many types of nerve cells and how many different muscles are involved in learning a new dance. Not only does the brain have to decide what types of muscles must be moved—and then send a signal to move them—but the memory area in the brain has to remember the steps. Once the brain learns the dance, the muscles and nerves respond easily. Then, we can enjoy dancing without thinking too hard about the steps!

This is how we learn all new movements, such as walking, riding a bike, or even learning to play games.

To Find Out More

Here are some additional resources to help you learn more about the nervous system:

 **Books**

Ardley, Neil. **The Science Book of the Senses.** Gulliver Books, 1992.

Morgan, Sally. **The Human Body**. Kingfisher, 1996.

Royston, Angela. **The Senses**. Barron's, 1993.

Sandeman, Anna. **Brain.** Copper Beech Books, 1995.

Simon, Seymour. **Professor IQ Explores the Brain.** Boyds Mills Press, 1993.

Walker, Richard. **The Children's Atlas of the Human Body.** Millbrook Press, 1994.

Organizations and Online Sites

The Carnegie Science Center
One Allegheny Avenue
Pittsburgh, PA 15212-5850
412-237-3400

ExploraNet
http://www. exploratorium. edu/
Visit a constantly changing assortment of online exhibits presented by the Exploratorium.

The Exploratorium
3601 Lyon Street
San Francisco, CA 94123
415-563-7337
415-563-0307 (fax)

The Franklin Institute Science Museum
222 North 20th Street
Philadelphia, PA 19103
215-448-1200

Harvard Mahoney Neuroscience Institute
Harvard Medical School
220 Longwood Avenue
Boston, MA 02115

Museum of Health and Medical Science
1515 Hermann Drive
Houston, TX 77004
713-521-1515

Museum of Science
Science Park
Boston, MA 02114-1099
617-723-2500

An Overview of the Brain
http://www.btfc.org/adult/ achp3.html
Learn about the brain and nervous system through simple text and illustrations. Includes the senses, cranial nerves, and spinal cord, as well as the various parts of the brain.

Important Words

axon long fiber that sends signals from a nerve cell body

cerebellum part of the brain that controls balance and coordination

cerebrum largest part of the brain; it is the center of thought, feeling, remembering, and it controls muscle movements

contraction the action of squeezing together

dendrite tiny fiber that carries signals toward a nerve cell body

impulse signal or message that is carried from nerve cell to nerve cell

fiber slender threadlike structure

nerve cell cell of the nervous system with fibers that send and receive nerve impulses

paralysis loss of power or feeling in any part of the body

Index

(**Boldface** page numbers indicate illustrations.)

autonomic nervous system, 12, 17
axons, 24, 25, 30, **34,** 35, 36, **37**
backbone, 19, **20**
balance, 15
brain, 5, 6, 7, 8, 9, 10, **10,** 13, **14,** 15, **16,** 17, 18, 19, **20,** 21, **22,** 24, 26, 27, 33, 40, 41, 42
brain mapping, 18, **18**
brain stem, 9, **10,** 17, 19
breathing, 7, 12
central nervous system, 10, 12, **28,** 29
cerebellum, **14,** 15, 16
cerebrum, 13, **14,** 15, 16, 17
coordination, 15
dendrites, 24, 25, 30, **34,** 35
ears, 15, 27, 36
electrical impulse, 35
emotions, 8
eyes, 15, 27

fibers, 24, 25
heartbeat, 7, 12
knee-jerk reaction, 38, **39**
memory, 18, 42
motor nerves, 21, **28, 29**
multiple sclerosis, 36, **37**
muscle fibers, **29**
muscles, 19, 21, 27, 29, 38, 41, 42
nerve cells, **1,** 21, 24, **25,** 27, 31, **31,** 40, 41
nerves, 11, **11, 22, 32**
organs, 19, 27, 29
pain, 26, 40
paralysis, 21, 23
peripheral nervous system, 11
Reeve, Christopher, **23**
reflex, 38, 39
sensory nerves, 19, **28,** 33, **33**
speech, 18
spinal cord, 10, **10,** 11, **11,** 17, 19, **20,** 21, **22,** 22, 23, 24, 27, 40
spinal-cord injuries, 23
vision, 17, 18

Meet the Author

Darlene Stille lives in Chicago and is executive editor of the World Book Annuals and World Book's Online Service. She has written several Children's Press books, including *Extraordinary Women Scientists, Extraordinary Women of Medicine,* and three other True Books on the body systems.

The photograph on the title page shows a magnified view of human nerve cells.